SUDDENLY, THERE WAS AN OVERFLOW

Winning With Your Faith

Nashauna K. Manboard

SUDDENLY, THERE WAS AN OVERFLOW. Copyright © 2024. Nashauna K. Manboard. All Rights Reserved.

Printed in the United States of America.

ISBN: 978-1-958443-60-6 (paperback)

This book contains materials protected by the Intellectual Property Law. Any unauthorised reprint or use of this material is prohibited. No part of this book may be reproduced or transmitted in any form or by any means, electronic or mechanical, including photocopying, recording, or by any information storage and retrieval system without the prior written permission of DayeLight Publishers or Nashauna K. Manboard (Nashauna.manboard@gmail.com). Although the author has made every effort to ensure the information in this book was correct at press time, the author does not assume and hereby disclaim any liability to any parts for any loss, damage or disruption caused by errors or omissions, whether such errors or omissions resulting from negligence, accident or any other cause.

I would like to dedicate this book to my husband, Dewayne Manboard, and my two sons, Kymani and Josiah Manboard, whose love and support have been a tower of strength to me and the why to carry on.

TABLE OF CONTENTS

Introduction 7
Chapter One: Who Am I 11
Chapter Two: The Transformation 23
Chapter Three: Faith With a Purpose 29
    Winning With Your Faith 34
Chapter Four: Success at Your Expense 37
    Success Will Cost You 39
Chapter Five: Change is Inevitable 43
Chapter Six: Familiarity 51
Chapter Seven: Delay is not Denial 57
Chapter Eight: Lost Then Found 65
Chapter Nine: And It Came To Pass 73
About the Author 79

INTRODUCTION

To experience an overflow will come at a huge cost to you. You must be willing to pay a substantial amount of faith to experience the Promised Land. It will cost you your family and friends. It will come at the expense of you being unliked and misunderstood. It will take you from a place of comfort to a place of unfamiliar territory, and there may even be some tears at times. It is okay if the journey costs you; it is okay if it comes at an expense to you or even takes you into unfamiliar territory, which brings about great pain. You must be determined and dedicated to fully embrace who God has endorsed you to become because of the directives upon your life. In your season of transitioning to your overflow, you cannot afford to compromise what is inside you because what is in you is necessary for the ones you are called to serve.

Here I am, in my early forties, with huge expectations for my life—being assertive of who I am called to be and what and where I am called to possess. Someone who knows me may be reading this and say, "You have achieved so much already. Is there anything else for you to achieve?" That is it right there! I know with every fibre of my being that there is so much more for me to achieve, and I have barely scratched the surface of what I can personally accomplish. I know that God has promised me the expected end, and in knowing this, I continue to press towards the ultimate goal which is to become everything God has ordained over my life.

What fascinates me the most about wanting more for myself is that there are others who feel the same way I do but refuse to get up and dominate. It is a human tendency to stay in a comfortable position because they have been doing the same things year after year. They have been going to the same places and never dare try to go somewhere different. As a society, we have become conditioned in our minds to live from a place of lack because we fail to do anything new. We have also conditioned our minds to live in our circumstances due to a lack of fear and self-doubt when the reality is that there is so much more that you possess that is waiting to come out.

Some of us are called to bring others out of captivity to a place of freedom, from a place of brokenness to a place of wholeness, and from a place of lack to a place of abundance. However, if you don't know who you are and what you possess inside of you, you will remain in a state of flatlining. This causes you to be in a high voltage of stagnation and allows you to succumb to who society wants you to be instead of becoming who God created you to be. So many choose to become people-pleasers and have lost their identity in doing so. Becoming unstuck from a place of flatlining, a place of stagnation, and a state of people-pleaser paralysis will require a new mindset. Apostle Paul reminds us that we must be transformed by the renewing of our minds so we are able to prove what is acceptable and the perfect will of God concerning us (see Romans 12:2). Renewing of the mind allows you to interpret life through the lens of God's Word and the inspiration of the Holy Ghost, rather than seeing through the lens of your own experience, woundedness, trauma, preferences or the opinions of others.

How does one strive to be persistent while pivoting and pursuing excellency in a world that allows you to be average? I recall, quite some years ago, a vision where I was in a room with directors, managers, and staff who were educators within the children's workforce sector. In my vision, the question was asked, "Who wants to pursue to extend in the field?" In my vision, there were others moving forward and wanting more, but I was comfortable where I was in business. How could I possibly go any higher? After all, God had blessed me with a business I did not ask for. Could there be more for me? A few moments after watching the majority moving forward and deciding to pivot and pursue, I woke up out of my vision and heard a voice say to me, *"Greater is in me."* Those words occupied and engrossed my mind and certainly left an impact on me—"Greater is in me!"

What in the world was God communicating to me? I soon figured out what that meant as I journeyed to the overflow. This book is for those who are willing to go the extra mile to experience the overflow that God has promised, even in the midst of facing adversity, trials, testing, and an economy in recession. Growing up, I would often hear, *"Hard work and determination is the key to success."* As I became older, I realised it was not just hard work and determination, but there was a key element that took quite some time for me to figure out as life became weary and rocky. It was my consistency that caused the hard work and determination to evolve. What if I told you that your faith must be accompanied by consistent work? Faith requires a lot of work, and consistency in your work will produce the outcome, which is your ultimate goal.

Can I let you in on a little secret? Faith is hard work! Winning with your faith is not something you pursue today and expect bingo tomorrow. It is certainly not something you say with your lips and with your heart you profess something different. Stick-to-it-tiveness is required to win with your faith. It is the ability to persevere even when all that confronts you tells you to give up. It is the ability to hold on to what God says instead of what you can see. The thing is, you only need a small amount of faith to dismantle, disconnect, and demolish everything that does not align with the promises of God concerning you. Wow! Talk about dismantling, disconnecting, and demolishing, in this book, you will get proven strategies while gaining introspection of how to truly manifest the trajectory of your life. This book will allow you to make quantum leaps with your faith instead of accepting your present circumstances or choosing to be content with what life has to offer.

Embark with me on this journey to discover in detail the producing of the OVERFLOW. Right now, your life may not have allowed you to reach your full potential. You may have settled for things as they are now rather than seeing things the way God sees them. The time has come to change all that. This book is for those who are willing to take risk in order to change the trajectory of their lives. I pray and hope that this book will impact your life, causing you to transform and transcend into everything that God has ordained over your life.

I also want to express my profound gratitude to you for taking the time to read this book. I am grateful for your commitment and honourable loyalty. Let us continue to elevate and evolve together while inspiring others to fully embrace who God has called us to be.

Welcome to the OVERFLOW!

CHAPTER ONE
WHO AM I

"Acknowledging who I am in order to apprehend my purpose."

When I was a little girl, I was always timid, shy, and reserved. (Who would have thought this?). I was never the one to be in front of the crowd or voice my opinion. If I ever had anything to say, it would take me quite some time to build up the courage to speak up or speak out on something, even if that thing was detrimental to me.

I lived in a small District called Watermount, which was located in the parish of St. Catherine, Jamaica. My parents were Christians; in fact, they both played active roles in the church. Church played a dominant role in our lives back then and still does. My parents, Oscar and Beverley Blair, had five children between them. They later adopted a son. I was the eldest girl and the second of their children. Being the eldest girl meant I had to do most of the house chores. Mum had her children, then went back to college to complete her studies as a teacher. My dad was a cabinetmaker at the time.

We grew up in a small two-bedroom house that included a veranda and living room. The kitchen and toilet were located outside. Our house was always welcome to visitors, family, and friends. How my parents managed to find space for everyone to feel welcomed, only God knew. Having five other siblings meant we would often have to share as there were times my parents could only afford the minimal, so on many occasions, I would mutter, "Oh, I wish my parents only had two of us. This would allow me to have more rather than having to share." That was my selfish thought then. Now I would not change my siblings for the world.

Growing up, Dad was very fixed on us having a relationship with God. I recall the early Sunday morning devotions where he had us singing out loud and reading the Bible. As kids, we clearly did not want to be singing out loud and reading, especially so early in the morning, but our dad made it clear to us and left us no choice. My dad was a strict Christian parent, while my mum ensured we took our education seriously. We were balanced on both ends. Mum taught at the same elementary school my siblings and I attended. Lucky for us, we managed to escape her class. I soon left for secondary education where I started my high school life.

I attended a mixed boy and girl secondary school located in Spanish Town, St Catherine. Secondary school was great to begin with, until the third year. That was when school and life became complicated for me. There were moments at school that I was picked on and even called names and made fun of. There were certain areas within the school compound that I would dare not cross over because I was afraid. Some days, I didn't want to go to school. I didn't tell my parents or siblings how I felt at the time. Looking back, I wish I did. This was quite painful at times, but I kept pushing through. Finally, I made it to the end of my secondary school, graduated, and, within two weeks, migrated to the United Kingdom. I knew for sure that I was ready for a new chapter in my life.

In 2000, I migrated from Jamaica to the UK at the age of seventeen, hopeful for a better future and a new chapter in my life. I left my parents and siblings behind. My sister came with me but only for the summer holidays, after which she returned to complete her studies at her secondary school. *It was a whole new world; a new fantastic point of view. No one to tell me "no" or where to go or say I was only dreaming.* That was how it felt. I soon began settling into a whole new world with endless possibilities, but unsure of what possibility to pursue. I enrolled in college to pursue a diploma in hairdresser. The college tuition was expensive because I was an overseas student. This would also grant me a student visa, allowing me to work in the UK. Being an overseas student meant that I would have to pay for all college tuition which came at a great cost. I had to get a job to pay my tuition. I got a job working in a take-away shop in the evenings, including weekends. Later, I got a job working as a trainee hairdresser.

I eventually got used to living in a new country and, by that point, I realised that moving to a whole new world with endless possibilities was going to be harder than I ever imagined. This was never a fairy tale, but it was place where if you really wanted to succeed, then you must think beyond the norm. You must be prepared to go above and beyond what is deemed acceptable within our culture, society, and environment in order to become who God has created you to be. Going above and beyond for anyone reading this will not be an easy road, especially when denials, doubt, grief, insecurities, and guilt confront you daily, contradicting what the Word of God says concerning your life.

I completed my year at college and was looking forward to my final year. This was proving quite difficult. I had built up a debt in my college course, and that would jeopardise my status in the UK. I had two choices: quit and go back to Jamaica or carry on, hoping that things would work out for my good. I honestly don't know how I managed to survive, but looking back at the outcome of my life, I know there was a greater power at work within me that was sustaining me. Two years after migrating, I completed my college course.

Some months passed after finishing my college course. I was offered full-time hours at the salon. This was great, but it meant my student visa was going to expire pretty soon. What in the world was I going to do next? Paying tuition was not the cheapest, and I had just barely finished paying for my tuition course. There was no way I was going through that again. I then made the decision to join the British RAF and went in search of how to apply. After seeking information on how to join the RAF, I was told that due to my student visa coming to an end, the RAF would not accept me at that point. I needed to apply to immigration to extend my stay. After a few months of waiting to hear back regarding my visa, I was told that it was unsuccessful. I felt disappointed, dismayed, discouraged, and was left depleted. This was meant to be the open door to solve my immigration status, but I was knocked down instead. How was I going to make it through this?

Sometime after, I met this guy. I had actually met him previously, but this time we both had a chance to introduce ourselves. He was very handsome and definitely an eye candy. We both had lots of things in common, and speaking to him meant I could be totally me. We dated for about five months and, to be honest, we got on cool, but he wasn't ready for a serious relationship. I could sense it, and I wasn't going to allow him to make fun of me. I did the impossible! I told him that he wasn't ready, and it was not fair on us both, so we parted. I didn't know that speaking up for something that I believed in was meant to be so heartbreaking. It broke my heart to say goodbye. How can one say goodbye to a love that was meant to last forever? "It was certainly love but *it is over now,*" I kept singing to myself. Only God knew how I felt.

Days turned into months, and about six months after we parted, we talked for the first time. One day, after finishing my shift at the salon, he gave my best friend and I a lift home as it was raining. He asked if he could come and see me again that evening. I said okay. We did this a few evenings after work, and spending time with him made me confused again. What should I do? I questioned myself repeatedly. He certainly wasn't ready six months ago; how would he be ready now? I didn't want to regret getting in a relationship with him again only to walk away, so I consulted my sister and best friend. They both told me to give him a chance. So, I took a risk. I thought, *What do I have to lose?* Yep, that was it, so we carried on dating.

Once in a lifetime, you finally find the one you love. *Can he be for real?* God must have spent a little more time on him for me. He soon became my best friend, companion, shoulder to cry on, and a tower of strength. A year and a half later, we were married. We were young but sure about our love for each other. I don't think we knew the extent of what we were doing when we said, "I do." Looking back, we were so bold about our love, even if others doubted.

Life as a married woman soon proved to have its ups and downs; the good, the bad, and the ugly. This was going to be hard work and not just a fairytale. There were moments we had to agree to disagree.

After a year and a half, we decided to try for a baby. We tried for quite some time, but nothing happened. This was heartbreaking at times. To make it worse, I was teased by my sister who called me "barren Karen." I felt like giving up on every chance of becoming a mum, but there was something in me that kept trying. So, I aligned my body in position and began taking my vitamins while staying in great health. One day, after doing a test, we had the results we had been waiting for. We were over the moon and could barely believe our eyes. I had a little life growing inside of me.

Suddenly, There Was An Overflow

My pregnancy had its ups and downs, but I enjoyed every moment of it. Being pregnant made me realise that God was always by my side; even when I left Him, even when I gave up on Him, even when I refused to stick to His Word, He was always knocking on my heart, and as I drew closer to God, I suddenly realised that He was drawing closer to me. Nine months later, I gave birth to a beautiful and healthy baby boy weighing over eight pounds. After years of trying, we are now parents. Let me encourage anyone on this path to becoming a parent; never give up on your dreams. Dreams will only come true when you decide to activate your faith and make it work.

A few years had passed since I applied for my stay in the country but we had no reply. The thought of not being able to work while awaiting the permission had proven to be unbearable. I had sleepless nights; crying myself to sleep had become the norm for me. I was slowly slipping into depression, but *who do I talk to?* I felt embarrassed at the time to even pour out to anyone.

My husband was our main provider, so he worked every day, including some weekends. Looking after a baby and not being able to have a balanced work life can be suppressing when all I did was stay in most days. If I can be totally honest, I was so close to committing suicide. There were days when a voice kept telling me to end my life. I looked at my baby boy at the time, and all I could see was his bright eyes staring at me. *How could I possibly leave him without a mother?* I felt depleted, distraught, distressed, and had lost control over my thoughts, allowing the enemy to steal my momentum. While he was doing that, he disturbed my peace. I began feeling insecure and became unintentional about my marriage. I didn't know what to think, expect or do. One day, while at home feeling paranoid about my entire life—including my marriage—God spoke to me and said, "I have brought you together for a purpose." Somehow, those words resonated in my spirit. I didn't want to lose my husband. God said "purpose," so I began pondering His words.

As soon as my husband came in, I confessed how I was feeling and that I began to think and feel like we had rushed into marriage too soon. I told him what God told me that day, even though we had no idea what God was talking about. So, I decided to get my act together. I heard "purpose," and that was all I needed to fight for my marriage and the love we both shared. Looking back at those moments of my life, especially the moments when I contemplated suicide, gave me the tenacity to keep excelling, keep working on me, and to always believe in myself. I often use this statement, *"If the enemy couldn't take me out then, what makes him think he can take me out now?"*

During those months, I started taking my relationship with God more seriously. I began seeking and praying more. I realised that God was the only one who could get me out of the pit I was in. I also made a decree and declaration that I was going to proclaim a fast. I told Him I would fast every Wednesday until He came through for me. From then on, every Wednesday, I fasted, and this went on for over a year. I was persistent, I was consistent, and I was determined to fast. I knew that one day, God would show up. I also made a promise to God that if He came through for me, then I would surrender my life totally to Him.

One Wednesday at about noon, as my fast came to a close and while I was praying in my room, I suddenly heard a voice whisper, "Your prayers have come through." I stopped praying and looked up, but there was no one else in the room with me but my baby. I knew it could only be God. With tears streaming down my face, I could barely open my mouth. I began to muffle, "Thank You, Lord."

Suddenly, There Was An Overflow

In less than an hour after hearing those words from God, my phone rang. I looked at it. It was my lawyer. My heart started pumping so fast, and my hands were shaking. I answered the phone. He confirmed that I had received my letter from immigration confirming my stay in the UK. What I had been waiting on for four years had finally come to pass, and it was unravelling right before my eyes.

My mess had turned into a message for me. What was taunting me had turned into triumph. You may be reading this and wondering, "What is the message?" The message for me is that God will never lie. He will never give you a promise and fail to deliver. It didn't matter how long I had to wait; He had to fulfil His words.

I went back to the salon to work part-time. My son had started school, so I needed to work around his school hours. It was great being back at work. I started doing driving lessons as the route that took my son to school consisted of two buses. It was quite difficult at times, but I kept pursuing it with the help of my husband. He took me out in his car, ensuring that I had enough practice. Finally, I was ready to do my driving test. On the morning of my test, I was very anxious and nervous. The Word of God tells us not to be anxious about anything, but in everything by prayer and supplication with thanksgiving, let your requests be made known to God. And the peace of God, which surpasses all understanding will guard your hearts and your minds in Christ Jesus. (see Philippians 4:6-7). I began to worship on the morning of the test as I journeyed to take my son to school.

After we got off the first bus, we then went on to the second bus and we sat down. Still worshipping, I suddenly realised something very unusual. A lady came over and sat right in front of me, and on her right shoulder, I saw the word "VICTORY" tattooed. With tears streaming, I said "Thank You, Lord." I knew that victory was certainly mine. Indeed, I passed my driving test that morning. God has again granted me my request. What more do I need Him to do to prove that He loved me and He cares?

There was a baptism scheduled to take place at the church. The thought came across my mind that I had made a promise to God to surrender my life to Him if He came through with my immigration paperwork but somehow, I had managed to convince myself that He might have forgotten about my promise. No, He did not. Never make a promise to God that you cannot keep. God does not forget our promises to Him and, of course, He kept His word so I should do the same. In August 2010, I made a declaration in front of God, my family, and friends that I was ready to follow Jesus. I certainly didn't know how I was going to do it, but I needed to do what I said I would have done. I must admit, at the time, I had no idea what God was preparing for me. I just knew I had to keep my side of the bargain. When I made the decision to follow Jesus, all hell broke loose over my life. My husband had a near-death experience on more than one occasion. This was very disturbing for us, and I was more convinced that I needed Jesus more. Almost two years later, my husband gave his life to Jesus.

One day, as I was in my house, I heard God say, *"See, I told you I brought you together for a purpose."* Hearing those words again for the second time brought tears to my eyes. Our destiny was formed way before we came into existence. God had it all planned out, and His plans are good and not evil—to bring us to that expected end (see Jeremiah 29:11).

Two years into my journey with Christ, while in my kitchen, God began to speak to me and show me some things. What He said to me was certainly unexpected and, at that point in my life, I felt I was clearly not ready. I even convinced myself that it was the devil making me believe things. *Why would God want to use me?* It had not been long since I started my faith journey, and I was still working on me. My dress code was somehow not appropriate for the calling, and neither was I ready for that. Why would God want to use me as an evangelist? How dare I think God would want to use me like that? I was not one of the choices in church to call upon to do anything. I struggled with those thoughts for weeks.

The more I struggled with accepting the call, the more God spoke to me. I was annoyed with God. I told Him to use all the other names I would call out to Him who had been in church for quite some time, and they looked the part. The more I did that, the more God was still stalking me. Well, that was what it felt like. One day, after being annoyed by God, I said these words to Him, *"If You are speaking to me about all these things, then confirm it."* I didn't want to hear anything else from Him until I had received some confirmation. I was serious about my statement to Him. A few days after, it was Sunday, and I went to church. After church, as usual, the pastor greeted the congregation as they exited the church. In all honesty, I usually try to find an escape route to avoid speaking with him. Sometimes we run away from the very person whom God has placed in our life to push, propel, and position us for our next.

As I tried to escape, he held on to me as he was already speaking to someone else and said, "I need to speak with you."

"Here we go," I said to myself, but I waited until he was through speaking. He took me to the office and showed me something. It was not what I expected to see and hear. *Hold on a minute. Did I not ask God a few days ago to confirm it for me?* I had tears streaming down my face; Pastor looked in astonishment. I told him how God had been speaking to me for weeks, and I was living in denial. I did not think I was good enough to be used by God. I did not think my life was perfect to be used by God. I didn't think I was a Christian long enough

for God to use me. In the Pastor's office were some candidate names for the Ordination Service. I saw my name at the bottom as an Evangelist. I accepted the call but lived in denial. A few months later, I was placed in an evangelism and church planting course. Again, I accepted to go on this training but still struggled to come to terms with who God had called me to be.

The next day, after I arrived at the training centre, I visited the rest room. While approaching the bathroom door, there was a sign on the door. The words on the door completely changed the way I thought about myself. It was so powerful that it shifted my entire life. It said, *"God doesn't call the qualified; He qualifies the called."* From that moment, my thought process regarding being an evangelist changed. It was then that I truly accepted the call.

"You can never transform your life until you position your mind to be in a place to receive."

We tend to think we can plan or mop out our lives the way we think it is supposed to be. We often think living a life of purpose doesn't exist for us but only exists for the upper class; therefore, we end up living in the land of lack and scarcity when the Word of God tells us that He gives us the power to obtain wealth (see Deuteronomy 8:18). The ability to hear God's voice and make the decision to transition and transcend requires dedication, determination and one being unapologetic about their intentions.

KEY REMINDER

"You can never transform your life until you position your mind to be in a place to receive."

CHAPTER TWO
THE TRANSFORMATION

"When there is no transformation, there is no progression."

Becoming the person God has called you to be will require a transformation. One's mindset must be renewed in order to progress and activate the new.

One night in September 2013, after attending a two-day conference, I had an encounter with the Lord during three days of fasting. He gave me a vision and clearly gave me some instructions. It was a confirmation of what took place at the conference I had attended. I sat and listened to the distinct voice of a young lady who seemed to be the same age as me. As I sat and listened to her in the conference room and how she spoke with conviction, I had a thought running through my mind, *"Oh, I wish I had the confidence and boldness she has to stand in front of an audience and speak like that."* Listening to her activated something in me. It activated a boldness I never thought I had. It activated me wanting more for me, and it certainly gave me the courage to relentlessly pursue more.

After a few years working at the salon, an increased feeling of apathy was certainly present. I felt a lack of interest in my job, like there was so much more in me and something was missing. Have you ever been in a situation where you felt that this was not all there was for you? It doesn't matter how many times you try wishing that the feeling would just go away; it remains. God sometimes allows you to experience a dry and uncomfortable patch so you become hungry for more; then He tells you to go for more. In one of my favourite scriptures in the Bible, God gave the children of Israel permission to accomplish what they never had, but because of fear, doubt, and refusing to take a leap of faith, they never received the promise.

After receiving the vision and instructions God gave me that night, I had to step out in faith. The land was set before me, and all I needed to do was go in and take possession. It wasn't the moment to allow fear and procrastination to consume me, but it was a moment when I needed to take my faith to a greater dimension. The next day, I told my husband what God had spoken to me. He was pretty excited for us to venture out into the field of business but was unsure of the location where God told us to go. God told me to launch a Children's Day Nursery. On the night of the vision, I told God I had no money. How could I possibly start something as big as that with no source of funds? All He said was that He would supply all my needs according to His riches in glory (see Philippians 4:19). If that wasn't bad enough, when He gave me the instruction of where to go, I told God no. Why would God ask me to start the business there? He knew it would prove quite difficult for me and my family. My husband told me no. He said we were not going there. That evening, I said, "Well, that was the instruction given to me."

A few weeks later, we approached our local council to pursue various buildings we could launch in. This proved unsuccessful for us. We had to go back to the vision and instructions God had given to me. We approached the bishop of the church and told him the vision and where God told me to launch the business. We also had a meeting with other representatives of the building. A few months later, after getting permission, we decided to make a start. With all the excitement of starting a new business, we had a surprise to our adventure. We found out that I was three months pregnant with our second child. We certainly knew how to choose our moment.

How could I be pregnant, especially at a time as crucial as this? For days, I had many thoughts running through my mind. I wished it had happened at a later point as starting a business and growing a little one inside of me at the same time just didn't seem to go hand in hand. *Who told you so? Who said you can't do them both?* Maybe the time had come to change all that, and it started with me. At that moment, I was capable of achieving new heights, set new standards of accomplishment, and was ready to make a quantum leap. We started making plans for the new baby while making plans for the new business. This was quite difficult and challenging. With God on my side and my husband backing me, that was all I needed. I can do all things through Christ who strengthens me (see Philippians 4:13). This was me rephrasing and putting into context what must have been one of the most complex times of our lives.

In May 2014, the business was up and running, and a little one was growing inside my tummy. I hired a manager in order to help with the day-to-day running of the nursery. We had no children to begin with at first, which was quite discouraging. In a few weeks' time, we had three children. Things did not add up, and I kept asking God, "Where are the children?" He spoke to me and said, "They're coming." This was difficult to process as I could clearly not see any children coming. All I had to hold on to was that they were coming. Let me reinforce this nugget with you; when God gives you a vision, the vision will not always be plain. The vision will sometimes not be pleasing, which causes you to doubt the fact that it was God who gave it to you in the first place, and it is not you running with something that was never intended for you. But, hey, in your season of waiting for it all to come together, I want you to be encouraged that God is not a man that He should lie, or a son of man that He should change His mind in regards to what He promised (see Numbers 23:19). Stay focused on what He said and not what you see, while anticipating that God's Word concerning you will come to pass. The manager assisting me with the day-to-day running of the nursery handed in her resignation and failed to turn up to work the following week. I was left distraught, dismayed, and felt depleted. We worked hard to put things in place, and now I was back where I had started. With no assistance at the time, I quickly had to recruit a manager and staff for the position. My baby was due in just over a month. *"Phew, no pressure God!"* God is our refuge and strength, always ready to help in times of trouble (see Psalm 46:1).

I managed to recruit someone we knew who was looking to start their journey in childcare. We were still without a manager, and this was a desperate call for help. Weeks had passed, and nothing changed. Our baby was soon to arrive. I worked throughout my pregnancy. There were days when I felt like quitting. I had a thousand reasons why I should quit and one reason why I should tenaciously pursue the vision. I kept going because the vision wasn't something I saw in a fairytale movie. The vision wasn't something inherited or given to me by my parents or descendants. It was a vision God gave me to run with. When we run with a vision, we will encounter obstacles, hurdles, and huge barriers to our success, but the key thing to adapt derives from a question I asked God when I felt like giving up. He said, "I didn't say it was going to be easy, but what I promised you is that I will be with you always." The key here is that God knew everything I was going to endure in accomplishing the vision. He is not shocked by the obstacles, hurdles, and barriers we face. What we need to focus on when we get to that point in our lives is that the plan of God is to prosper us and not to harm us, to give us an expected end (see Jeremiah 29:11), so with all the obstacles, hurdles and barriers I was facing, God had my back and He certainly had me in the palm of His hand.

In August 2014, one early Tuesday morning, I gave birth to my second son. Who could it be but God? It was only by His grace and unmerited favour upon me. While in the birthing room, I told God I had no energy to push the baby through. I had worked through the pregnancy and only had the weekend to prepare for the baby. I felt His grace; I felt His power, and I felt His presence shining down on me as I pushed my baby out. He came pretty quickly without any complications. I was out of the hospital in just over five hours of giving birth. I wanted to stay longer so I could rest, but there was no chance of that happening. Mother and baby were doing great, and they needed the room as beds were short. I was soon home with our baby. While trying to enjoy our new arrival, I had to quickly bounce back into work. My husband got laid off from his job just before our baby was due, so he was there to support me both at home and at the nursery.

We were drained financially and physically. All we had to hold on to was our faith. With me having to return to work, Mum came from Jamaica to help look after the baby while I was working. This brought tears to my eyes most days. Having to leave my newborn for over ten hours each day was devastating.

Some time had passed after doing some recruiting, but we couldn't find the right candidate for the job. We had to do something about the issue we were facing or face closing. After having a conversation with our local authority that Wednesday evening, we had to make a decision the following Monday; that was pretty daunting. All we could do was pray, trust, and believe. We closed the nursery on Friday for the weekend, not knowing what we would do on Monday. On Saturday, I received an email asking if I would consider them again. This email came from one of the candidates we had previously offered the job but who declined the positioned a few days later. I could barely believe what I was seeing in the email. God showed up in three days! He was on time; always have, and never late.

To my reader, don't you dare give in to failure. Failure will only become an option when we give in to the cares and pressures of this world.

What had proven to be impossible became possible. God can do all things, but there is this one thing that He won't do and that is fail. Keep believing for the impossible. The manager had settled in; we had new staff, and new children were coming in. I could take a back seat to the nursery and finally enjoy my baby. Mum's six-month vacation with us ended, and I was back to looking after my baby full-time. He came to nursery with me on the days I worked. Finally, things were starting to fall into place. Business was blooming, and my husband was now working. We had made a decision that it was time to pursue our home as we were paying rent and had been in that accommodation for over ten years. It was time to take our faith to the next level. Speaking of faith, this journey to our new home was the biggest faith-test for us. Our faith was tested, tried, and then transformed. It took us on a journey where our feet had to walk upon the water and trust that God would deliver on His promises, even if He had to break down the walls of Jericho.

KEY REMINDER

"Failure will only become an option when we give in to the cares and pressure of this world."

CHAPTER THREE
FAITH WITH A PURPOSE

"If you say that you have faith and then forfeit the work, then you are only professing, which produces no progression."

Do you trust that the trials, tribulations, and trauma you are facing are simply preparing you for one of the most significant breakthroughs of your life? Stay with me on this journey of faith. In this chapter, you will hear how I went from trauma to triumph and from trials to transformation.

Now faith is confidence in what we hope for and the assurance about what we do not see. (Hebrews 11:1).

In 2016, we decided that we wanted to become homeowners. This was by far one of the most devasting experiences in our lives. We decided to step out in faith, but it cost us! "How can faith cost you?" one may ask. When you decide to step out on what is known as crazy faith, it will come at a huge cost. Crazy faith in God produces an unshakeable and unwavering tenacity in you, which also allows you to be confident in the fact that, after you have suffered a little while, the God of all grace, who has called you to His eternal glory in Christ, will Himself restore, confirm, strengthen and settle you (see 1 Peter 5:10). In the process of stepping out in faith, we lost the home we had been renting for over ten years and were left homeless. The embarrassment and humiliation of having nowhere to live with two children could have only brought us closer to God. We handed in our notice to our landlord, hoping to have our new home processed and ready. In acknowledging that we were almost homeless, we had to secure another month from the landlord and hope that things would work out or, as a last resort, we could rent another accommodation until things had sorted out. Three weeks into having an additional month from the landlord, we began searching vigorously, hoping to secure a rented accommodation.

We viewed numerous properties and made large quantities of applications, including paying a deposit, but everyone came back to say we did not pass the security checks to secure the rented property. By this point, I was beginning to lose my faith. I felt like God was punishing me. *Can God punish one for stepping out in faith? How can this be if God's will for our lives is for us to prosper and be in good health? How can a believer not walk into the prosperity, wealth, and abundance that was promised?* We questioned God. We were left depleted and ran out of options on what to do next. We had money in the bank, but we were declined every possibility to stop us from becoming homeless. We soon figured out that being submissive to the will of God for our lives was the only way out and forward. When we learn to be submissive to our journey, our tests and trials, we then understand that nothing we have been through was wasted. The tree, which represents our faith, was planted, and in order for the tree to survive, we needed to water and nurture it. For you know that when your faith is tested, your endurance has a chance to grow (James 1:3). The four weeks additional notice period ended, and the landlord refused to extend our time any longer as he had a tenant waiting to occupy the house. We had to put our furniture, clothes, and other possessions in storage. We took a few pieces of clothing items for a few days with us.

We handed over the keys to the house to the landlord while unsure where we would sleep. We both looked at each other as we drove away in separate cars from the premises. My husband looked over at me from his car with tears in his eyes, and all I could barely whisper and say to him was, "God will come through for us." *What on earth had we gotten ourselves into?* I blamed myself for pushing my faith to the next level and causing my family to be in that position. We drove off to a car park. My husband needed to go to work that day, but I had a day off, and it was also the summer holidays. We called a B&B accommodation and checked ourselves in. They asked us how long we intended to stay; we told them a few days, then continued to extend each week.

During this time, we only told a few close family and friends that we had nowhere to live. We felt so embarrassed; we dared not let this get out to the public. We continued our life the same; we went to work, our eldest was back at school, and our youngest accompanied me to the nursery. Living from bags and not knowing where life would take us next brought our relationship with God closer. We only had one room in the B&B. We prayed and mostly kept the television on the God Channel to strengthen the journey we were on. God will sometimes create a season of uncertainty, a season of what feels like a mess in our lives, in order for us to transcend into our destiny. Rest assured that in your seasons of uncertainty you have a lesson to learn. Don't ignore the lesson; attend to what is been taught, jot down some notes, listen to your instructions, and trust the teacher that He knows best.

Let worship become your posture. I recall on a few Sundays at church, I had to lead praise and worship with the thought of nowhere to live; nowhere to call home. A song reminded me in that moment to forget about ourselves and worship Him, and that was all we could do. As I began to not focus on the problem but on the one who is the problem solver, I was convincing and urging the congregation to worship God and to give Him the glory He deserves. I had to give God my true worship. When you begin to usher true worship to the Father in times of hardship, it doesn't eliminate the problem, but it certainly brings you peace so you can rest in your storms. God is seeking out true worshippers who will worship their way into their promise. Yet a time is coming and has now come when the true worshippers will worship the Father in the Spirit and in truth, for they are the kind of worshippers the Father seeks. God is a Spirit, and His worshippers must worship in the Spirit and in truth (see John 4:23-24). No one knew what we were facing. We felt humiliated, ashamed, and embarrassed, plus the fact that we were facing eviction from the B&B as the manager had realised we seemed to be living rather than passersby.

If we didn't have enough on our plate to handle, the manager at the nursery handed in her resignation, and within two weeks, my staff, who worked closely with the manager and myself, also handed in her resignation. *How can one worship while going through the fire? How can you keep a posture of praise when it feels as if your whole world is crumbling apart right before your eyes?*

Worship is an homage or respect paid to God. Your present situation should never affect the worship you give to God but should be a conduit of how your worship flows. By the time church was over, we quickly ran off to avoid anyone asking us how we were or suspecting our situation. The time had come to leave the B&B, and we only had a few days left there. We could not stay any longer, and it was becoming unbearable for my kids and husband. For me, it was my safe place as we had nowhere left to go. My husband decided to go and seek help. We were told that the only place they could offer us was a hostel where they housed the homeless. At this point, I was still pushing my faith. I told God He could do better than that. Refusing to live in a homeless shelter, we went to our local council and told them our situation. We told them we had money for rent, but everywhere we tried said no. They promised to help us.

The next day, my husband received a call that a property had come up and if we wanted to see it. My husband went and viewed the property with our eldest son. They came back with big smiles on their faces and said it looked okay, but it needed work. He had signed the contract immediately for the place and would collect the keys the next day. Our eldest said, "Mum, we have a garden!" His little face said it all. They could now play outside without anyone telling them that they couldn't. The keys were ready the next day, and all the paperwork were signed. I then visited the property for the first time. I recall walking in, looking around, and seeing the state of the property. It was all falling apart with mildew all over the deteriorating walls. My husband turned and looked at me to see my reaction. I turned my eyes up towards heaven and said to God, "Is this the best You can do for me?" There are moments in our lives when God will allow us to go through tests, fires, and hardships to see if we will still stand by His Word. I had my plans, but was this truly God's plan?

We tried to rent fine, luxurious properties that I thought I deserved. Still, the only available one that was successful was the one that was unsuitable for living accommodation, according to my standards. That moment felt like all hell broke loose, and spat out what was left on the table for me. All I had left in life was to gather the crumbs to make bread for me and my family. I soon had to come to terms with our new home while living on faith with a purpose.

We tried our best to do some work to make it suitable for living conditions. Months passed, and I felt the call of God on my life for ministry. I was set forth by my pastor, so I surrendered to the call. The call of ministry was non-negotiable, regardless of how my life was.

Suddenly, There Was An Overflow

In September 2017, I started ministerial studies. I took on the role of manager at the nursery, but working full-time was very difficult at times. I recall journeying to North Hampton after work on Friday evenings, trying to beat the rush hour traffic to arrive on time for training. My husband and kids often accompany me when on training. It was so important that they understood the process of my calling and that they were involved just as much as I was. Many times, when we are called into ministry, we often leave our closest and dearest ones behind to accomplish our studies. This can often lead to neglect and major disruption in the family. It is important for us as ministers when we are called to understand that it is not just one person within the family that is called; the calling is on every individual in your household. Having my husband and kids with me every step of the way was encouraging and proved rewarding.

I don't know how I did it, but God made a way for me. With the hustle and bustle of managing and directing a full-time business, being a wife and mum, and having various roles in church, I often felt overwhelmed. There were days I wanted to quit, hide, run away, and just be me, but my husband, kids, and closest family kept pushing me to stay the course.

During the time living on the acquired property, the living conditions began to deteriorate. We went through a time of rat invasion to hundreds of flies along with other creatures seeking refuge in the house. We knew this was not normal and that we were in spiritual warfare. This was certainly a distraction, but we continued to stay strong in the Word of God and trust that He was making a way for us. Our only way upwards was to seek God daily.

Winning With Your Faith

In July 2018, my husband received confirmation from God to start the procedure for our new home. This could not have come at a better time. Before we could proceed to pursue the house, we had to honour God with a seed. My husband had made a promise to sponsor a pastor who was going on missionary work abroad. God reminded him of his promise and told him that he needed to fulfil it. We sowed the seed by sponsoring the flight for the missionary that same day and believed that God was going to fulfil His promises to us.

Two weeks after sowing the seed, God spoke again to my husband and gave him instructions for us to get in touch with our mortgage advisor, so we followed His direction. Things went pretty quickly, and we were soon house hunting. We found a house by August, so we proceeded with the paperwork. While doing all that, in the same month, I had my commissioning service for my ministerial studies. This was a huge accomplishment for me and my family.

Let me take this time to encourage someone who is on this journey or you are thinking of commencing your journey. When you take care of God's business, then you will have no issue seeing God take care of your business. I could have waited until God gave me a better home, but I listened to His call, and even in the midst of my pain, sufferings, disappointments, worries, rejections, and fears, I answered the call of God on my life, choosing to obey rather than sacrifice. Someone reading this might be asking, "Then why do you have to sow? Why do you need to give?" This is a biblical principle that seedtime and harvest is God's method. When you sow into God's kingdom, then you will surely reap a harvest. We certainly did. We moved into our home in October and saw the hand of God mightily making provisions for every detail of the house. Everything we needed, His hand provided, and He certainly gave us the best. *"Great is Your faithfulness, Lord unto me."* We reaped a harvest in the same year we sowed.

Isaac planted crops in that land and reaped a hundredfold the same year because the Lord blessed him. The man became rich, and his wealth continued to grow until he became very wealthy (see Genesis 26:12-13).

KEY REMINDER

"When you take care of God's business, then you will have no issue seeing God take care of your business."

CHAPTER FOUR
SUCCESS AT YOUR EXPENSE

"There are many reasons why we should quit, but one reason why we must keep going."

While growing up as a little girl, and even in my early teens, we were taught that great success comes from working hard at school and achieving good grades so we can get a good job. But what is a good job? Someone may have gotten good grades in school, went to university and landed a job in the field of medicine, while another barely scraped through high school, then college, but turned out to be running a six or seven-figure business. How do we measure success, especially for the younger generation coming up? In a world where the younger generation seeks to be successful and requires it the quick and easy way, it is important we educate them that success does not come quickly and easily; it comes with hard work, dedication, consistency, and faith. But how do we apply our faith to be successful?

God has given us everything we need pertaining to life and godliness (see 2 Peter 1:3). I recall hearing this scripture for the first time and meditating on the first line of the text. I came to the conclusion that the power was already in me, and the promise was already granted to me. If God has given me everything I need to pursue who He has called me to be and to walk in the fullness of it, what then is stopping me? Did you know that the key to success is also in the decisions you make? I want to pause here and rephrase this question. *What is stopping you?* We can often be the biggest obstacle to ourselves. We often wait for others to invest in us. We wait for others to see the goodness in us, and we seek their approval daily instead of believing what the Word of God says concerning us. You were created to be the head and not the tail, above and not beneath, the lender and not the borrower. In 2019, I felt a shift in my life; it was time to come out of my cave. God gave me a vision, and in that vision, He wanted me to empower women from all walks of life. This was a new mantle given to me and one that was going to require a new me. I needed to step out in faith with God as my consultant.

Earlier that year, when I felt the shift in my life, it left me feeling and wanting more. There was a vacant room in my life that needed filling. I began searching and seeking God for direction. I knew there was more in me, but what was it? I prayed for quite some time, and while praying, there was all kinds of ideas coming in my thoughts. I was ready to walk into this newness that God had granted me. I started doing my first ever motivational talk and was getting ready to do my first YouTube video. One Sunday, during a conversation with a company director, he told me how he had been away on holiday. It was not just a holiday but more of a business adventure. He said he learnt a great deal while abroad. *"This sounds interesting,"* I thought to myself, but what did he learn? Whatever it was, I was desperate to learn it too.

I went home that evening and prayed to God about what He had mentioned to me. I told God that I needed Him to reveal what it was I needed to hear so I could move into my next. I fasted and prayed about it and waited for God to answer. During the week, I received a message from the individual I had spoken to. He told me in the message that he was refusing to give me any information, but the Holy Spirit kept prompting and convicting him to do so. He told me about a training he had booked to attend out of town, and he gave me the link. I knew God wanted me to attend that training. I spoke with my husband and we both agreed to attend the training; my sister agreed to look after the kids for us.

Success Will Cost You

The weekend was very impactful with various speakers. We took so much away from that weekend and felt the need to enroll in another training event weekend. This was going to be the start of something incredible. Not only was it the start of something incredible, but we also knew that we had to invest in ourselves. Yes, dear reader, success will come at a cost to you. When we decide to fully walk in the entitlement that God has planned for us, yes, it will cost, but we must be willing to invest in ourselves. Now, here is the thing that I learnt on my journey: I learnt that if you don't invest in yourself, then don't expect anyone else to invest in you. A few weeks later, we attended another training in London. We were very excited about what God was about to do. The training was everything I wanted and nothing I expected. I learnt so much and had so much work to put in. I kept doing more training and relied on God for direction at every step of the journey.

In November 2019, God spoke to me about going live on Facebook, proclaiming the Word of God. This was daunting, and I felt like I wasn't ready to go live.

What if I messed up?
What if I didn't sound right?
What if the people didn't receive me?
What if... What if... What if... must have gone through my mind over a thousand times.

I was scared and nervous and kept procrastinating. By December, the holiday season had come, and I was off work for a week. Within that week, all that kept going through my mind was that I needed to go live. I mentioned it to my husband, and he replied by saying, "If God tells you to do it, then you must do it." With my husband and God in my ears, it left me no choice. I decided to go live one Friday at 8 pm. Leading up to the live, all nerves kicked in, lashed at me, and I was ready to quit. Luckily, my husband was not having it. He got the lighting, PA sounds, and everything ready for me while I got dressed. I came downstairs, and I was frozen. As I sat down in front of the camera and looked over at my husband, all he said was, "You're live!"

I saw that I was indeed live, so I began speaking.

It is important that we choose a spouse who is able to align themselves with the call of God for our lives. Doing that enables us to walk in the fullness of our calling without trying to compromise the call.

After finishing the live, I knew it was my calling. I felt relaxed and was able to speak freely as the Holy Spirit led me. I started going live with the Word of God every Friday night with my husband playing some gospel music in the background. It was called "Hour Power." I had worked really hard over the months leading up to that moment, investing in myself, and it was the time to put everything I had learnt into action.

At the beginning of the year 2020, I already had the vision. I had planned my first ever in-person conference in April and was looking forward to it. The event was called "How to Become a Better Wife." The venue and speaker were secured, and promotions and ticket sales were on the way. In March 2020, we had some devasting news about a global pandemic. Everything, except the Word of God, had to come to a standstill. I had no idea when I could proceed with the conference.

I closed the nursery during this period and found myself, for the first time, having a break so I could spend quality time in the presence of God. Hearing from God during the weeks and months had proven refreshing, renewing, reaffirming and I was ready to re-establish my calling. It was exactly what I needed. I started going live more on various social media platforms and was certainly building my confidence. I continued with "Hour Power" every Friday night, and it was proving quite popular during lockdown. When God gave me the instruction to go live in 2019, little did I know that the world was going to face a lockdown that would force more people to be on social media and I never imagined that three months after starting "Hour Power" that the world would change to a new norm of being on social media.

When God gives you a vision, you must run with that vision. You will never know what is tied to your obedience. Being on social media prior to lockdown had boosted my confidence and was a great foundation for what God was preparing me for in the coming months. God spoke to me shortly after and told me it was time to launch out and start mentoring women from all walks of life. I developed a six-month mentorship program for women who needed to build their confidence and gain clarity on their purpose, vision, and goals. This was a great success for me. I met with the ladies once a week online and did weekly catch-up sessions with them individually. From the six months mentorship, some of the ladies went on to start their own businesses, others had seen huge success in their businesses, and some had a boost in their confidence enough to go on to build their own speaking platform.

In late 2020, God gave me a vision to start a Christian clothing brand called FaithWorks Fashion. He told me that He was giving me a platform to spread His Word. This prophesy was first spoken over my life in 2013. I thought about commencing, but it looked way more challenging than I expected, so I kept putting it off. One day I decided to make a move and start. I had to take some time to learn this new business adventure but I gave it my all. It took me quite a while to really understand the process, but I kept trying until one day I started printing. I planned the launching date for January 1, 2021, and was pulling all the strings to get this accomplished, and we did.

In January 2021, I launched my clothing brand, FaithWorks Fashion. God, You are good, and Your mercies endure forever. When one decides to surrender everything to God, allowing Him to be totally in control of your destiny, then you will begin to see the manifestation of His glory upon your life. You don't need to chase it; it will overtake and overflow your life. I don't speak because of what I have been told about God but I speak because I have witnessed Him do miracles and wonders in my life.

KEY REMINDER

"When one decides to surrender everything to God, allowing Him to be totally in control of your destiny, then you will begin to see the manifestation of His glory upon your life."

CHAPTER FIVE
CHANGE IS INEVITABLE

"For change to become known, you have to be willing to be uncomfortable."

Why change?

In a world that is constantly changing, change is inevitable. It is paramount that we embrace doing things in a different way than the norm. By refusing to do so, we face the possibility of remaining in the uncomfortable situation that we are used to, which causes things to remain dormant in our lives. Have you ever wondered why some people walk in the fullness of their calling while others refuse to shift? The reason is because of CHANGE. Research shows that one in three people avoid change if they can. One of the most profound things about change is that it takes you out of your comfort zone. It allows you to rely on the not-knowing rather than the knowing. We also know that great things do not exist in comfortable positions. If I am too comfortable, then I am not growing, and in order for me to evolve, I need to be uncomfortable.

I experienced major changes in my life in 2022. God shifted the trajectory from what I least expected. This did not just involve myself; my entire family had to experience this shift. Transitioning was one of the biggest challenges I faced in 2022. It felt like I was in a strange and foreign land, and I found myself questioning the will of God for my life. It is not that I didn't trust Him, but I felt nervous and overwhelmed about what He was doing. God had big plans for me, but was I ready for my next? Of course, it took me out of my comfort zone, but I was willing to confront all my fears and give it a go. Change is necessary for God to upgrade and expand you. The question is, do we want the upgrade as much as God wants it for us? Many people want the upgrade but tend to move slowly towards it because of fear or doubt or in case it doesn't work out. They are giving it a slow and cautious pace.

Joseph had to experience major changes in his life to reach the palace. From being thrown into the pit to managing Potiphar's business, he had to embrace the suffering, the season he was in, and the shift that God was about to initiate in his life. Joseph might not have fully understood his assignment when God gave him the vision, but what Joseph was certain of was that he was going to stand and say what his God was saying concerning what was to come. Sometimes the vision will not always be plain; it will not always come with a blueprint, but the concept of having a vision is that you make a move until you hear your next. So many of us have gotten visions from God, but because we didn't get all the evidence—the blueprints, the next move, the how's and the when's—we fail to start, not realising that we can only get our next when we step into our now. I feel this will help someone as you are reading right now: *"You will only get your next when you step into your now."*

Have you ever felt different from your siblings when you were growing up? During my younger years, I could recall that something was different in me. It almost felt like I was the black sheep of the family. I could not explain what was happening in my life, but I felt different. It was unexplainable. I couldn't discuss this with my parents because I didn't understand what was happening to me. I couldn't find the words to describe how I was feeling anyway. I recall hearing from God at a very young age and sensed that my path was going to be different. Joseph knew that he was somehow different from his siblings. Being different sometimes can be like the odd one out in the family or a black sheep. Growing up amongst his brothers, Joseph had visions from God which was going to promote him, but somehow his family did not believe in his vision. There are moments when God will give you a vision, and your own family members will not believe in your vision, but that is okay. The vision was not a conference call from God. The vision was given to you, and only you can run with it at the appointed time. You must be confident in God's vision and trust His plans.

If Joseph hadn't embraced the change he was facing, he would not have been in a position to make huge provisions for his family during the famine. The transition to who he became was not easy for him, but he persevered through all that came to confront and disrupt his life. Joseph survived what would have been a murder case when his brothers thought they would sell him instead. How do we remain humble, even when we are dragged through a pit and when no one believes the vision God gave us? Joseph had to resist the urge to conform in the midst of his transformation. He remained focused on the promises of God rather than getting distracted by the plot and snares of his enemies.

When God gives you a vision, the enemy's job is to wipe it out. He will cause you to abort the plans prematurely before you even get to the birthing room. The goal is to endure the full stage of labour. While you are about to give birth, you will also need to evaluate who you are taking with you into the labour room because not everyone will be happy to see your new baby. Not everyone who calls themselves a midwife is actually one. You must have a spirit of discernment, especially in your birthing season, when you have a vision to run with. In your season of transitioning, you must be able to recognise a murderer from a midwife and an assassin from an assistant. An assassinator of your destiny will always present himself as an assistant to your destiny. But how does one detect an assassinator from an assistant, you may ask. This is not always easy as they appear like sheep. But the Word tells us that we will know them by their fruits. What are they saying, and how are they reacting to you when you begin to move forward? Are they encouraging or are they very negative? Are they optimistic with your visions, or are they a pessimistic to your vision? Now these are only a few of the things that I used to detect assassinators trying to enter my life. Above all, I ask God to direct me and give me wisdom. I rely on the Holy Spirit to instruct me when I am unsure.

God's will for us is to walk in the prosperity He has promised, but we get to decide how we do it. He gives us free will but also gives us the tools and wisdom so we can prosper and be in good health.

God will sometimes allow us to go through a season of rejection or isolation so He can refine us. Dealing with any form of rejection or having to isolate for any given period can often seem detrimental, but when you understand that the isolation or rejection was only a redirection into your purpose, then you won't mind being in that position. It comes only to shift you into a greater dimension in God. You may be going through your season of rejection or isolation and feel like the world is against you; I want to encourage you by saying, "Chin Up." What they meant for evil concerning your life, God will use it to bring His glory to you. Just like Joseph, the evil against him was never meant to destroy him. It wasn't about Joseph, but it was about the people he had to help. God will allow you to fall for you to gain.

You may have fallen while in the process of birthing your vision; you may have gotten some limbs fractured along the way or shed some tears, but let me say this from the rooftop: you are about to walk into your greatest season because what was meant to frustrate, antagonise and cause you to quit on God's promises will only redirect you to your promised land. But don't wait to see the promised land before you believe God's promises concerning your life; you only need to BELIEVE. Joseph believed in his God and went from obscurity to certainty, from the pit to the palace, and from the least to the greatest among them.

How did I embrace change to fully walk into my God-given assignment? First of all, it was a very uncomfortable period in my life. There were days when I didn't want to be me. I felt rejected, misunderstood, and unsupported, but you have to understand that during your period of transitioning, there is a grace and beauty in being rejected, misunderstood, unseen and unsupported by people. It teaches you not to rely on anyone but to rely on the source, which is God. I had to learn to embrace who God has called me to be. When you learn to master that, then you will understand that your assignment is mandatory. Some people get frustrated during their transition. They are frustrated because of the process they need to endure to get to the finish line. You are never alone because there is always somebody else going through what you are facing, but you must remain focused because the enemy will come with distractions to take your focus and vision away from the promises of God. Someone may be asking, "How do we become focused in a world where there are so many distractions?"

Paul wrote these words to the Ephesians: "Be very careful, then how you live, not as unwise but as wise. Making the most of every opportunity, because the days are evil. Therefore do not be foolish, but understand what The Lord's will is." (Ephesians 5:15-17).

In the year 2022, distractions confronted me and disrupted my flow. I could barely focus on anything. I started questioning God. I needed help. I needed to have something that could help me navigate my day-to-day assignments. I felt as if I was here, there, and everywhere, apart from what I was meant to do. God spoke to me one day and told me that I was going to create a system that would enable me to focus more. I doubted this for months as I thought that it was way above what I thought I was capable of doing. We were heading into the last quarter of the year, and I still had not made a move on the vision God gave me.

I felt ill in October and was off work for a few days. During my time off and away from work, God began to deal with me. I had no choice but to make a start. He gave me a name, and I began to work. The whole process from writing, designing, and processing took me two months, so it was out in time for Christmas. When God gives you a vision to run with, you better run with it. You will only understand the whole vision when you are prepared to obey God. What I thought was far beyond what I was capable of doing became second nature to me.

I need to help you comprehend the greater being that is placed within you. When the Bible speaks about doing "all things," it simply means ALL—All meaning All. You can do all things through Christ who strengthens you (see Philippians 4:13). For there is greater that is placed within you than what is in the world. I doubted myself. I didn't think I was capable of doing what God asked me to do. I asked God to show me something or even someone who had created this system before so I could purchase it. He told me that I was going to produce my own system and, of course, I did just that.

In December 2022, just in time for the new year, after delaying what was already placed within me for months, was now *The Purpose Planner*. I was pleased with myself and all my accomplishments. The Purpose Planner was designed for you to be intentional with your purpose, vision, and goals. Since creating and using The Purpose Planner, it has been and still is helping me to plan purposefully while staying focused on my goals.

KEY REMINDER

"You will only get your next when you step into your now."

CHAPTER SIX
FAMILIARITY

"Familiarity will allow others to resent the new version of you."

We often become so familiar with things and, therefore, we begin to take them for granted. We tend not to celebrate them as we once did and even quit noticing them. Have you ever wondered why the people who were once close to you reject who you are becoming? The reason for this is familiarity. They knew who you were. They knew the old version of you but resent being introduced to the new version of you. They knew when you had little or no confidence so all you did was rely on them…They knew when you barely had anything, and all you could do was live on the streets of lack and scarcity…They are the same ones you once trusted with your secrets, so they are still holding your past hostage, and because of familiarity, they cogitate that you are not qualified enough to bring them to a better place in their lives, so they continue to seek out others rather than hear what you have to say.

What encourages me about familiarity is that Jesus also experienced it and still went on to do greater works, even though they did not receive Him. I had a profound revelation when I realised that the real jewel of life is not the comfort in knowing that people will always be cheering you on; the real jewel lies in knowing that God will always be cheering you on. The purpose of our assignment is to shine for men to see what God has done and what He is doing in our lives each day. In the same way, let your light shine before others, so that they may see your good works and give glory to your Father who is in Heaven (see Matthew 5:16). Too often, we allow the "I knew you when" from others to keep us in a state of stagnation, which can be cataclysmic to our purpose. The Word of God tells us to shine. This is where we often neglect this word. We often fear that if we shine, then it could come across to someone who is feeling insecure about who they are, as if we are bragging. We fail to shine because shining could make others uncomfortable or even feel threatened by you. When we fail to shine, then we begin to fail God. If shining allows your associates to leave you, then you weren't meant to be associates in the first instance. My instruction to you is to SHINE. Don't you ever stop shining. By doing this, it is pleasing unto the Lord.

Would you change the fact that you are no longer the same person they once knew? The answer for me is no. I had a conversation with God regarding the world of familiarity, which causes people not to see and accept who we really are and who we are becoming. He replied in the most profound way and said, "You can never CHANGE what they think about you, but you can CHANGE what you do about what they think about you." Other's expectations and assumptions of me lies in how I handle it. I can choose to keep on evolving or choose to accept their rejection. *"I choose to EVOLVE."*

Choosing to evolve will exempt you from being in everyone's circle, but with God it is not a requirement. It is not a requirement to be in their circle to fulfil your purpose and destiny. Neither will anyone's inner circle dictate your purpose. Your purpose is solely dependent on God. Before you were conceived in your mother's womb, God already had a plan for your life, and that plan was certainly to prosper you and not to harm you, and to grant you an expected end (see Jeremiah 29:11). That expected end is a promise to you, and you will need to align yourself with the right people and environment in order to accomplish that expected end. Even though the promise is to you, it requires that you take the necessary steps to fulfil that promise, even if it causes you to experience some form of loneliness; even if it causes you to be rejected and despised. You have a responsibility to ensure that you are purposeful in your heart to carry out every God-given assignment on your life. The Apostle Paul was not in Jesus' inner circle, yet he was deemed one of the greatest Apostles of all time. Paul knew what was placed inside him, and he was able to fulfil his purpose.

How can we ensure that familiarity does not hold us hostage? I was asked to preach at my local church some years ago. I asked God what He wanted me to say to His people. Sunday came, and I went up nervously and gave the undiluted word of God to His people. The word was not gladly received by many of the congregation, but it was exactly what God gave me. We had a guest speaker the following Sunday. He went up, announced the topic and started preaching the word of God; it was exactly what I gave the people of God the previous Sunday. While listening to the preacher, I heard loud amens, claps, and hallelujahs. A thought came to my head, *"Is this not what I told you last week? Yet, I barely got any amens, claps, and hallelujahs?"* This is exactly what familiarity is! People become so familiar with you that even when the word is beneficial to them, they will turn a blind eye to it, while others will refuse to hear you out. My question to you is, *"Will you continue to speak the word of God even in the midst of rejection?"* I sure did! It wasn't easy knowing that my very own did not appreciate me, but I had to grasp the concept that the anointing placed upon my life is not about everybody cheering me on, but it is about me not compromising who I am, who I am called to be and what God has placed inside of me.

Living a relentless life for God will allow you to be carefree about what others say, think, and do about you. They may want to hold you hostage to your past or try to convince you that you are not good enough due to where you are coming from or who your relatives are. If you choose to allow someone else's familiarity of you to hold you down, you will be in a state of flatlining, which will demolish and disintegrate your purpose on earth.

Can you handle the discomfort in knowing that they do not accept you? Can you handle the fear that will creep up every now and then that they do not perceive who you are? I had to find myself by knowing what the Word of God says about me. I had to quote and believe in the Word, that this is what God says and not what man says. When I found myself in the Word, and the Word became the reality of my life, then I was able to handle the discomfort of familiarity. Too many people forfeit their purpose because they cannot cope with the discomfort familiarity brings. There are many who choose to return to who they used to be just to be able to fit into a circle or a group they have outgrown. God desires for us to become who He has created us to be. If it means you no longer fit in, you no longer have their friendship, you no longer can sit at their tables, then so be it. You must be intentional and deliberate about who you are and who you were created to be. You have outgrown their limitations and expectations, and it is time for you to rise.

You are necessary for this season. Jesus was necessary but was never accepted in His hometown, even though He had the greatest intentions for their lives. They just couldn't see beyond who He was and where He came from. They questioned everything He did, and so He charged them that whosoever received Him, to them He gave the power to become the sons of God (see John 1:12). If we consider the things we see and hear in the world we live in, we can become so familiar with who our God is that we tend not to see how great He is. We can get so familiar with Him doing the small stuff in our lives that we tend to devalue the big things He can grant to us. Familiarity can keep us in a place of stagnation, enabling us to be jealous and even envious of others.

Moving past familiarity will allow you not to misappropriate your blessings. If you are struggling with familiarity, keep doing what you are called to do. They may refuse to accept what God is doing and what He has done in your life, but you have to become that person and move beyond *"I knew you when..."*

KEY REMINDER

"You can never CHANGE what they think about you, but you can CHANGE what you do about what they think about you."

CHAPTER SEVEN
DELAY IS NOT DENIAL

"At your appointed time, it will happen."

Why does it feel so difficult when waiting? Many years ago, I asked God to help me relocate my business. It felt like it was now time to venture out. I prayed and fasted about it and was convinced that God was certainly going to grant me my request. Sometime later, He spoke these words to me, *"At the appointed time, I will make it happen."* This was certainly not what I was expecting God to say. In fact, I thought He would have granted my request. I thought God was going to show up for me like I was His favourite girl. I thought He was going to make it happen for me, so I felt very discouraged and dismayed. It almost felt like God owed this to me.

Now if you have ever come across me, you would know that I am an advocate for sowing. I believe strongly in the principle of giving and reaping. For several years, I have been sowing seeds and paying tithes for my business, so when God said that to me, I felt like God owed me what He had promised. He told me to prove Him and see if the windows of heaven would not open and a blessing would be poured out to me.

Where is the favour God promised me when I brought my tithes and seeds into the storehouse? Have you been there, where you expected your sowing and tithing to manifest in your situation, especially when the pressure has been applied? How do you truly activate patience when it feels cataclysmic, which is detrimental to your health and well-being, spiritually and physically? All I heard from God was, *"At the appointed time, I will make it happen."* The devil wanted me to give up on God's promises regarding my business, but somehow, grace allowed me to keep going. During that time, I felt hopeless like the man at the pool of Bethesda, who had been in his condition for thirty-eight years. Every time he got up to move to the water so he could be made whole, someone always got there before him. This must have been a very frustrating time of his life, sitting down, waiting for his next, and then watching others get their next. Here's the thing; we serve a God who specialises in making the impossible possible, regardless of how long you must wait or how long you have been down in that position. When God tells you to go somewhere, He expects you to stay there until He gives you further instruction. Staying in that position can and will allow you to experience storms, drought, being misunderstood, and even cause you to be persecuted, but you must maintain your posture and stay put. God knows when it is the right time, and He certainly will perfect that which concerns you at the right time.

This biblical illustration given in the Bible of the man at the pool should change our perspective of waiting our turn. Years had passed and this man continued in his situation. I guess he was waiting for his moment, but even in our moment, God will watch to see if our faith will work. After Jesus listened to this man's reasons for being in his condition for so long, this was His response to him. *"Jesus said to him, Rise, take up your bed and walk. And immediately the man was made well, took up his bed, and walked." (John 5:8-9).* Was he really going to get up and walk after being in that same position for over thirty-eight years, or was he going to doubt after all those years of being in the same situation? So, I had to wait my turn. The phrase "at the appointed time" informs me that there will be a specific and appropriate time when God will perform it.

How do we handle waiting on God? Do we give up on our assignment and begin to sing the songs of lullaby while throwing a pity party, or do we continue in hope so the power of God may rest upon us? I was in an uncomfortable season and had to make myself comfortable in God's promises. I couldn't see it working out, but it was the knowing for me that if God says so, He will bring it to pass. I became determined while being persistent like the widow who went before the unjust judge. Her persistence caused her to get his approval. This woman's rights were being violated, and she wanted justice for her adversary. So, she kept going back to the judge pleading her cause. When you are determined and persistent with your faith, God will always show up. He is moved by your determination to see what He said come to pass. I continued in prayer to God.

The suffering activated a demand on who I am and what God has placed within me. I continued to wait until my change was ready to reveal itself. God is a God of times and seasons. The ultimate goal is to remain patient while having an expectation that God can and that He will, while having the assurance that He is faithful to His promise. Years passed, but still, there was nothing from God.

In 2022, when I first produced the purpose planner, one of my visions in the planner was to have a new place for my business by April of the same year. I put in place steps to achieve that goal. April came, and nothing happened. In fact, some months after, I went through a devasted season within my business. My entire world had collapsed. Everything I had laboured so hard for in my business was crumbling right before my eyes. There were tears and more tears. Someone who was meant to be supporting me and my business had become an antagonist to my business, causing us to lose a lot of revenue. For days, I remember weeping before God. Once again, my faith was tested and tried.

Was God trying to bring me to a place where I knew that my only hope was in Him? Was everything that I had faced preparing me for the shift that God had for me? Little did I know then that it was. At my lowest point in those days, when I felt depleted, my husband took control of the situation. He began to pray and cover his family. During that time, God gave my youngest—we call him the prophet—a prophetic word for the family. As he spoke in his usually cheerful way to us, I heard God through him that Sunday evening. My son said we should meet for prayer as a family every day for the rest of our lives, even on Christmas Day. Who thought that meeting together every day to hear from God, to glorify Him, and to spend time in His presence could have shifted us as a family and take us from glory to glory. Again, the suffering activated a demand on what God had placed inside of me. What was meant for evil concerning me had brought glory to God. The Apostle Paul, in his writing, encouraged us that when we face trying times, we should ask, "Who shall separate us from the love of God?" (see Romans 8:35).

As a family, we began to daily meet before God rather than our usual meetings once per week. We thought this would prove challenging, but somehow, we made it work. We looked forward each evening to meeting together and would always prioritise this over everything else. This was the groundbreaking point of our lives. We have been doing this well over a year now and I would urge everyone reading this book to make a pledge to commit your family to the Lord by spending time in His presence. It will keep you all together and in the power of God's might.

So, what's next? We continued to wait patiently for the Lord, having an expectation to receive from Him what He had promised. When you can handle the discomfort of waiting, then you will be able to handle your purpose in God.

In 2023, God told me that He would perform an overflow in my life. As I approached the beginning of the year, I made sure to get my visions and goals written down in my planner. One night, the Lord visited me and told me that it was now time to launch out and start a ministry. He said He was trusting me with the responsibility of bringing His people a message of hope and that now was the time. This would also cause us as a family to relocate the ministry in which we served. This came as a shock to my family and myself. I knew it would happen someday, but somehow, I felt that the timing was wrong. I kept asking God if He was sure about this significant move in our lives. God assured me that now was the time. He had prepared my family for this by ensuring that we met each day to spend time in His presence. Six months later, God told me it was now time.

When God is about to perform a major shift in your life, He will always prepare you for what is to come. We had no clue why God wanted us as a family to meet daily until He told me to relocate and start this ministry. We started making preparations towards starting while allowing God to give us precise instructions regarding the ministry. There were days I wanted to give up even before I had ventured out. There were days when all I did was weep. The pressure and intensity of it all was getting to me. I expected encouragement from some of my elders in ministry and those in leadership positions, but I got little or no encouragement or support. It almost felt like everyone needed an explanation of what I was doing and what God had said to me. I told God, "I don't want this!" I never asked for it; I was very happy doing what I was doing. Throughout this time, He spoke one word to me, "Emmanuel," meaning God is with me.

Suddenly, There Was An Overflow

Who do I turn to for guidance? This was the question I asked God repeatedly concerning the ministry, but there was no reply. It is very unusual for anyone to start a ministry without having a minister or pastor to oversee them. The question was thrown at me, "Who appointed you?" I had only God as my appointer. He affirmed me, and that was all I had to hold on to. Many didn't believe in the ministry and still don't, but it is my obedience to God that matters the most.

The ministry was launched in March of the same year. We rented a place for the ministry for two Sundays each month, while we were online for the other Sundays. This started at a slow pace with some nervous waiting some Sundays as we were unsure if anyone would turn up or even support the vision God gave me, but we remained humble in the process and the small beginnings.

During our fifth month of ministry, I got a phone call one day saying that the building that we were renting had gone into liquidation, and we only had a few days. This came as a huge shock to us. We had only just started, and we found ourselves without a building. If God takes you out of something, it means He has something bigger and better for you. I told God I wasn't going through that process of renting anymore, and it was now time to purchase our own. I told God I needed somewhere big enough to accommodate my business and ministry. This is what I would call my biggest and greatest "Faith Move." Early in the year, God told me that my faith was going to get me the building. With this in mind, we started making preparations towards our faith.

We made inquiries seeking a property. There were not many suitable ones. I needed a place big enough to accommodate our vision. After all, I knew God was setting me up for something GRAND with everything I had been through with my business. When you have been through test after test, trial after trial, with the whole host of darkness coming against you, expect to see God in all His glory while being assured that the testing of your faith through experience produces endurance. This was going to be something grand, one that I had never experienced or encountered before. During this period, it felt like all hell broke loose. Things that weren't activated got activated against us, so we prayed, fasted, and cried out for God to bless us just like He did with Jabez.

Sometimes the only blockade to what we see is what we say…the only setback to what we experience is what we express…the only delay to our victory is what we verbalise…so, we cry out to God for help in order to demolish every dry bone within our territory and every high thing that goes against the will of God concerning us. And, it was so!

KEY REMINDER

"The suffering activated a demand on who I am and what God has placed within me."

CHAPTER EIGHT
LOST THEN FOUND

"The fight was always set for us to win, but many people lose the battle in the midst of the heat."

I didn't lose my salvation, but I had forfeited my HOPE during the heat of the battle. I was losing me! Can I keep it real with you? My entire journey to that place of overflow was not easy. There were days I just wanted to pack it all in. There were moments when I did not want to continue and felt that it was easier to give up and walk away from everything that God had promised. There were many days, in fact, weeks when I wanted to quit my business and the ministry that God had told me to start. I just wanted to become the girl who would hide away, sit in the back, and hope that no one would even notice that I was in the room. But God didn't want me to give up on me. He wanted me to fight the good fight of faith. He is a God who will go and chase that one sheep that has lost their way in order to bring them back to their purpose.

How think ye? If a man have an hundred sheep, and one of them be gone astray, doth he not leave the ninety and nine, and goes into the mountains, and seeks that which is gone astray. And if so be that He find it, verily I say unto you, He rejoices more of that sheep, than of the ninety and nine which went not astray. (Matthew 18:12-13).

Suddenly, There Was An Overflow

I may not have lost my salvation, but I sure did lose my hope in believing for the promise, but faith rescued me. Faith made a demand on me, gripped me, and made me hope again. But how do we continue to keep hoping for what we can't see?

For in this hope, we are saved. Now hope that is seen is not hope. For who hopes for what he sees? But if we hope for what we do not see, we wait for it with patience. (Romans 8:24-25).

It is imperative that we emphasise and make a statement in order to assist those who are coming after us, those who are in the same place as us, and those aspiring to walk in that overflow that there are days when you will not want to get out of bed and serve the people you are called to serve, whether this is in your job, business or ministry. There were days I wanted to throw in the towel and call it a day, but would that be effective for the people around me and those waiting for me on the other side? There were moments when I truly lost myself because of what I was facing, but I had to quickly find myself in those moments by dismantling and deactivating every feeling that was not in alignment with the will of God.

Dear reader, the will of God will never take you where the grace of God cannot sustain you. His will can never take you where His arms cannot support you, and His will never send you where the riches of God cannot be your supplier. In all this, God is our ultimate sustainer, supporter, and supplier.

This overflow I am sharing with you came with great suffering; it came with heartaches and discouragement. I faced repeated attacks, especially in the form of witchcraft sent to me, my family, and business. People I did not expect—including close family members—rose up against me while some refused to speak to me. When Paul said the sufferings of this present time will be nothing compared to the glory that will be revealed in us (see Romans 8:18), I felt like he had a revelation of me in glory, and in that revelation, he saw and knew that one day I was going to need this word that would whisk me back to glory. It would remind me that the tests and trials are working out for my glory. They would remind me that God has me in the palm of His hands, and He is working in the background so that when I become weak, the power of Christ would rest upon me. Even though the overflow came with suffering, heartaches, and discouragement, this was nothing compared to what God had prepared for me.

So, like the apostle Paul, I boast in my weaknesses; I boast in my pains and sufferings, and I will boast when they send attacks against me, my family, and business because in my weakness, God, who is the ultimate defender, the undisputed champion of all times, gets to step in and show that He is Lord of lords. He gets to demonstrate that no power on earth or schemes of man can ever pluck us out of His hands, and He gets to prove that He is our refuge and strength. The fight was always fixed for us to be triumphant. Jesus took the heavy blows, endured all the whipping, and managed to escape Accident and Emergency Department so that He could die on the cross for us to be victorious. That victory still stands! That victory is calling out your name and waiting for someone to walk right into it. Will it be you?

Nothing I went through was in vain. It was a setup! It was all a part of the plot to assist me in my victory. In the heated moments, I could not see the setup, nor did I notice that it was all a plot. When you are experiencing a fire, all you can see, sense, and smell around you is fire and smoke. You don't notice that the Fire Quencher is stabilising and sustaining every fiery dart of the enemy. I didn't see that God was not trying to stress me out, but He was stretching me, causing an erupting of an earthquake in me that would birth the overflow. Did you know that everything you have gone through has prepared you for the shift and the new thing that God is about to do in your life right now? The fire you faced, the embarrassment, shame, and guilt were all a part of the plot. It was all a setup for you to pivot into your given assignment. God knew exactly what He was doing when He allowed the fire to confront you. He knew the fire would have stirred up that prayer warrior in you. The fire would have stirred up the worshipper in you; the fire would have activated a new level of faith within you. So, no matter what you are facing, trust that God is using it to bring you through to your next level.

Everything I had been through propelled me into what I am experiencing right now. It propelled me into it because of the intensity of the heat. Many people choose to give up or throw in the towel because of the complexity of the process. They get mad at God for not showing up or taking them out of the fire. God's ultimate intention is not for anyone to be burnt in the fire; His goal is for us to come through as pure gold. He declares that when we go through the fire, we will not be burnt (see Isaiah 43:2). The issue is, do we trust God's Word that we will not be burnt when we go through the fire? And do we trust Him when we feel like we are drowning? Can we stay faithful in Him and ask Him to lead us where our trust is without borders? Can we say, as Peter did, "Lord, if it's You, command me to come to You upon the waters?" (see Matthew 14:28). Because it is the failure to trust God's Word why many give up or lose the battle in the midst of the fire.

The three Hebrew boys were placed in a fiery furnace because they refused to bow down and worship any other gods but their one, true and faithful God. They were fully convinced that their God was going to show up for them, and even if He didn't, they were still convinced that He is God and refused to bow to any other gods. This is exactly how God wants us to be confident in His power. He wants us to have that confidence that even when faced with persecution, tests, and trials, we are still convinced that He is and will see us through it.

The king ordered the fire to be seven times hotter, expecting that this would certainly bring them to ashes, but little did he know that our God is a Fire Quencher and He will quench every fiery dart of our enemies. If only the king knew that this same fire would destroy his men completely when placing the Hebrew boys in. Do you know that when you stand for God, He will show up in all His glory for you? This amazed King Nebuchadnezzar as he got up only to realise that these boys were still alive, and he ordered a release in their favour. Somebody reading this might be experiencing some fire. I bring you good news: God is about to release favour to you. The fire you are facing is activating favour on your life. You must experience this fire to activate the favour. Fire produces favour, and for you to see the favour, fire must be present.

How do we cope when we are constantly facing the fire? How do we keep going when the fire is under our feet? HOPE. Hope is a feeling of expectation and desire for a particular thing to happen. Hope is the confidence and assurance in the possibility for what we are desiring or longing for to happen. Hope is present and doesn't just appear out of nowhere. Hope is in our fire; hope is in our pain; it is in our discomfort and everything that keeps us up late at night worrying whether God is going to show up for us or not. Hope is always around and has never left you, but you must search deep within to find it. You cannot see hope, but it is the knowing that you have hope.

When you are on your journey to becoming who you are truly called to be, you must be prepared to walk every extra mile of the race to get to the finish line. There are no shortcuts, and neither are there any skipping lanes. Every hurdle, bump, and bruise comes with its learning goals. In every disappointment and bruise that I had faced, I needed to figure out what my lesson was. What was it that God was teaching me?

Suddenly, There Was An Overflow

Many years ago, I recall attending an evening service at the church. They had a guest speaker for the day. After he finished preaching, he made an altar call. I recall going up to the altar with a load of burdens and issues that I had been carrying for quite some time that would not shift from me. I felt like I was carrying life's leftovers, and the more I tried to get it off me, the more it kept oppressing me. While standing at the altar, the preacher came over to me and said, *"God is giving you a backbone."*

"Hold on a minute!" I thought to myself. I had been carrying these burdens and issues for quite some time now in the hope that any day now, God would release me from my struggles and pain. But all this preacher said was, *"God is giving you a backbone."* I certainly did not think I needed a backbone at that time, but looking back on my life, the backbone had stirred up a fighter within me that I did not knew existed. The backbone I thought I didn't need was the very thing that allowed me to walk in my victory. God knows exactly what you need to survive. He knows what you are able to carry, and He will not place anything on you that you are not able to overcome. When Job was facing his test and trials, he said God knows the way that he takes, and when He has tried him, he will come forth as pure gold (see Job 23:10). Even in Job's afflictions, he was sure that God was giving him a backbone in order to stand victorious over everything that satan was bringing to him.

Backbones are necessary for you to walk in your victory. A backbone is exactly what you need to defeat your enemies. You will need a backbone to stand when your feet thread upon new territory. When you are in the fire, you will require a backbone to get you through it. You will need a backbone to stand when life brings you disappointments, stress, and grief. So the next time you feel like giving up, remember that God is strengthening you by giving you a backbone in order for you to come out as pure gold.

KEY REMINDER

"The fired you faced, the embarrassment, shame, and guilt was all apart of the plot. It was all a set up for you to Pivot."

CHAPTER NINE
AND IT CAME TO PASS

"Congratulations!"

October was the month of deliberation for my family and me. I was led to a powerful and prayerful movement of prayer, praise, and worship. I began to research it, then decided to join in one night. I listened carefully to what the pastor was saying as he encouraged us to dance around in praise and thanksgiving. He explained the symbolic meaning of the dance. We shouldn't wait until we can see the victory before we sing and dance, but we sing and dance until we see the victory. I decided to dance around in faith, and as I danced, I felt the presence of God, and He began to speak to me. I continued to dance and anticipated joining in each night. Though it was midnight for us in the United Kingdom, I ensured that I joined in most days. These sessions were a powerful time of prayer, praise, and worship. During one night of the service, I began to worship, and as I uttered worship and thanksgiving to the Lord, the Spirit of God moved, and I couldn't hold back the tears.

SUDDENLY, THERE WAS AN OVERFLOW!

God threw open the doors of His sky vaults, poured out the scheduled rain on me, and blessed the work of my hands. What was promised by God had now begun to manifest. It came to pass that God remembered Nashauna Manboard, and every living thing, and all the cattle that was with me in the ark, and God made a wind to pass over the earth in my favour. *"Whew!"* It felt like I was in a dream. God opened major doors of opportunities for me that kept flowing over and over. It was the overflow that God promised me in November 2022. In a vision, He told me, "What's in my cup would produce an overflow."

You prepare a table before me in the presence of my enemies. You anoint my head with oil, my cup overflows. (see Psalm 23:5). All this time, the overflow was already placed upon me. God had already prepared the table for me. The tests, trials, and tribulations were activating an eruption of an overflow in the background of my life, and was waiting for the appointed time.

Who could have imagined that God would have perfected all that was concerning me and more. It was beyond all that I had ever expected of Him. If that wasn't enough, He then gave me these words, "I know your works. Behold, I have set before you an open door, which no one is able to shut. I know that you have but little power, and yet you have kept my word and have not denied my name." (Revelation 3:8).

What if I did not trust God's plan?
What if I didn't obey God to start the ministry?
What if I had sabotaged my blessings due to the naysayers all around me?
What if I had allowed what I saw to distract me from what He said?

All these thoughts and more came rushing through my mind. God is the ultimate Provider, the final Decision Maker, and the one who holds the keys to life. When God is ready to bless you, the barriers to living a successful life are removed, obstacles are dismissed, and all boundaries are eradicated. Everything I had been through was preparing me for that moment—a moment of truth and transparency, seeing God in all His glory.

Dear reader, there is absolutely no limit when it comes to God. There is nothing that He cannot do. There is no mountain that He cannot move. In fact, He can do ALL things except for this one thing, and that is fail. He cannot and will not fail you. Take Him out of your box and watch Him work miracles in your life.

Are you in a season of feeling overwhelmed? I want you to use this moment to do some internal inventory checks.

What is taunting your temperature?
What is agitating your atmosphere?
What is preventing you from your purpose?

Now, arrest your atmosphere with praise and thanksgiving. When you give God the praise that He deserves, you will see God's plan concerning your life being manifested before your eyes. We have the power inside of us to cast down everything that comes up against us. The devil attempts to make God's people feel overwhelmed in well-doing. He has been attempting to convince you that your efforts are ineffective, that your wisdom is being wasted. If you are on the brink of throwing in the towel, I want to encourage you that giving up is not an option. Do not get weary in well-doing for, in your due season, you will reap if you faint not (see Galatians 6:9). Your reward, restoration, and recompense are almost here. Do not allow what you see to get you distracted from God's promises concerning your life. God will never disappoint; neither will He discontent you.

So, what's next?

Suddenly, There Was An Overflow

Having done all to STAND, stand on God's promises. When you have arrested your atmosphere so you can respond to the call of purpose for your life, you need to know when to stand. You have done all you can, STAND; you have fasted and prayed about it, STAND. You have praise and worship your way through it, STAND. You have made the decision to trust God's plan, STAND. You feel stuck and unsure of what to do next, STAND. Is it always easy to STAND? The answer is no. You need to understand that you are not only standing but you will see the salvation of your GOD.

When Jehoshaphat came up against the vast army, God told him to "Stand still." (see 2 Chronicles 20:17). If Jehoshaphat had disobeyed this instruction, he may not have won the battle. God wanted him to observe what He was doing. Can you take a minute to STAND STILL and observe what God is doing in your life right now? He is bringing things to pass before your eyes. We often miss God in the moment because we fail to obey His instructions. In doing so, we can forfeit the promised land, even though we are so close.

What instruction is God giving you today? The ability to hear God's voice, even in an overwhelming situation, is paramount to your victory. As a matter of fact, it is the foundation of any victory you will receive in your life. You may ask the question, *"How can I hear God when all around me is chaos, cataclysm, and confusion?"* I have learnt over the years that finding a quiet environment or choosing to be alone to hear that still, quiet voice—instead of all the other voices that you are hearing—will allow you to focus and to hear God clearly.

It is said that for growth, success, and transformation to happen in your life, it requires you to be in a private space. I will share with you a little secret of mine. You can try this, and it might just work for you too. When I needed space away from the hustle and bustle of life as a wife, mum, pastor, boss and mentor, I usually told my husband and sons, *"Mummy is under construction."* It means I need some quiet time alone so I can speak to God while hearing from Him in order for me to be renewed and revitalised. Without this, I am unable to hear clearly from God as to what my next step is. My husband and kids laugh whenever I tell them I am "under construction," but it works for me. Sometimes, you must decide to put an end to the war of your emotions so you are able to embrace your destiny.

How did I end the war of my emotions, frustrations, and confusion?

One of the things I learnt about God was that He does BIG things when you begin to believe and call things that are not as if they are into your atmosphere. I used a picture of the building I was praying that God would bless me with as the screensaver on my phone and in my vision book. It gave me an opportunity to see it each day, especially in the moments when it felt impossible. Each time I doubted the promise, I would see the picture and my faith would be reignited that God was working it out on my behalf. I kept the picture for months in the hope that God would show up like He always did. I would rejoice with praise and thanksgiving to God every time doubt and fear showed up. In fact, I placed a demand on my life to worship my way through it.

One night, I had one of the most profound revelations about worship. That night, I was in so much pain. I started praying, but nothing changed. The painkillers I took were ineffective. A thought came to me, and I began to worship. As I worshiped that night, the pain suddenly disappeared. It wasn't a case where the pain decreased gradually; it disappeared instantly. As I continued to worship while reflecting on what had just happened, the Holy Spirit was teaching me something. There are some things in your life that prayer and fasting won't move, but when you begin to worship God in the beauty of holiness, you attract God's attention. You will then see God in all His glory.

I want to stir up the worshipper in you today. *What do you need God to do for you?* Go ahead and begin to worship. In fact, give God your best worship and watch God work in your favour.

As I continued to worship my way through to my victory, these words were cemented in my spirit, *"And it came to pass."* Oh, yes, He did! He came through in a way that exceeded all my expectations. He came through exceedingly, abundantly, more than what I could have ever imagined.

Isn't God amazing? He knows how to deliver a package that you have been waiting for. Isn't it powerful to know that God knows exactly what you need and when you are in need the most? I certainly take no credit for the victory I received. It was all God. He gave me the hope to believe that all things are possible when I truly activated my faith for it to work in my life. I am only a vessel He decides to use to reach others by encouraging and empowering them into the victory that God has planned for them.

If this book has taught you anything, remember this: *"Your faith will get you there."*

KEY REMINDER

"It's not what's in my cup stay in my cup, but it needs to OVERFLOW."

ABOUT THE AUTHOR

Nashauna K. Manboard is a licensed educator, entrepreneur, pastor, speaker, certified life coach, wife, and mother. She has a deep passion for children's learning and has served as one of the leading directors in this field. Nashauna humbly accepted the call of God upon her life as a pastor four years after she graduated from achieving her ministerial studies. She has a profound message for anyone who comes in contact with her that *"There is hope for those who are hopeless through the Word of God."*

As a certified life coach, she empowers both men and women on how to get in position so they can prosper in their purpose. Nashauna provides various coaching programs to help God's people become fully equipped personally, professionally, or prophetically. In this quest, she has composed *The Purpose Planner,* which is designed for you to get intentional with your purpose, visions, and goals so you are able to walk in God's plan for your life. Nashauna is also passionate about her approach to kingdom entrepreneurship and encourages the body of Christ to pursue entrepreneurship and take dominion over everything God has given us. It is her goal to continue to birth kingdom businesses such as her very own clothing brand, FaithWorks Fashion, and she is determined to enhance the kingdom of God in her creative designs of faith-based clothing and accessories.

www.ingramcontent.com/pod-product-compliance
Lightning Source LLC
Chambersburg PA
CBHW070518090426
42735CB00012B/2828